THE COOK-ZEN® COOKBOOK

THE COOK-ZEN® COOKBOOK

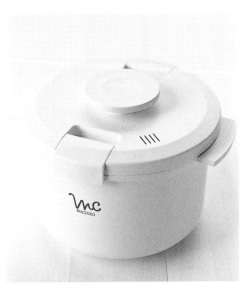

Microwave
Cooking the
Japanese Way—
Simple, Healthy,
and Delicious

MACHIKO CHIBA

LAKE ISLE PRESS NEW YORK

Published by:
Lake Isle Press, Inc.
16 West 32nd Street, Suite 10-B
New York, NY 10001
(212) 273-0796
E-mail: lakeisle@earthlink.net

Distributed to the trade by:
National Book Network, Inc.
4501 Forbes Boulevard, Suite 200
Lanham, MD 20706
1(800) 462-6420
www.nbnbooks.com

Library of Congress Control Number: 2007924524

ISBN-13: 978-1-891105-34-0
ISBN-10: 1-891105-34-5

Book and cover design: Liz Trovato

Editors: Pimpila Thanaporn, Katherine Trimble

Translator: Akiko Chiba

This book is available at special sales discounts for bulk purchases as premiums or special editions, including customized covers. For more information, contact the publisher at (212) 273-0796 or by e-mail, lakeisle@earthlink.net

First edition
Printed in the United States of America

10 9 8 7 6 5 4 3 2 1

ACKNOWLEDGMENTS

After ten years of dedicating myself to the creation of the Cook-Zen pot, I am extremely happy to bring it to the United States and to publish this book through Lake Isle Press. It is a great honor for me. Throughout this project I have received kindness and support from many people to whom I am grateful. Their warmth and encouragement have helped me to pursue my dreams. I want to thank the wonderful friends I have made while working on this project, and readers like you. It is my hope that this book will bring a smile to your face and warmth to your heart equal to that which I have received in writing it.

I would first like to thank my daughter, Akiko Chiba, who is actively pursuing a career as a pianist in New York City. Without her help in translating my Japanese recipes into English, this book would not have been possible. I realize how hard she has worked, considering the very different demands of translating and being a musician. Akiko's understanding of both Japanese and American culture, along with her willingness to try many of my recipes on her own, have allowed us to work together in harmony. The support of Pimpila Thanaporn, a wonderfully talented editor at Lake Isle Press, has also been greatly influential. I truly feel proud and thankful to have worked with an editor whose high ideals have led us to this point. Kate Trimble is another wonderful editor at Lake Isle Press. Thank you for your help during the photo sessions. Thanks also to designer Liz Trovato, for making this such a beautiful book.

Toni Brogan, our food stylist, began each day by choosing the freshest, most creative ingredients and who always took the time to beautifully prepare and present my recipes. Her assistant Greg Lofts is a wonderful stylist himself. His kind heart was felt by everyone in the kitchen. Stephanie Basralian, our prop stylist, used her imagination and personal taste to display my cooking so beautifully. I admire her determination and skill.

Photographer Tina Rupp not only amazed me with her talent, but with her warm personality as well. I appreciate the understanding and respect she has for her work and her co-workers, which is evident in each of her beautiful photos.

Mutual hard work and a wonderful team have made the creation of this book possible. The experience was a fulfilling one and, of course, it would not be complete without the key individual who brought us all together. Ms. Hiroko Kiiffner, president of Lake Isle Press, has put her faith in me, bestowing a once-in-a-lifetime opportunity to experience work in this country as a chef. I consider her a mentor and an advisor who has given me courage and pointed me in all the right directions. Her husband Calvin, an architect, was always present and made us smile. Thanks also to Nozomi Terao, who first introduced me to Hiroko.

I would also like to thank Ms. Saori Kawano, president of Korin, distributor of the Cook-Zen pot and other fine Japanese cookware. For the photo shoot, Korin generously provided us access to their excellent tableware collection. Without the teamwork of Ms. Kiiffner and Ms. Kawano, my dreams would have remained dormant in Japan. These wonderful ladies believe in me, and it is because of them that I am here today.

Finally, I thank my husband Toshio, a wonderful surgeon, my lovely son Keisuke, an enthusiastic and willing taste-tester, and my beloved cat, Tora. They always wait patiently for my return to Japan and I thank them for their support and unconditional love over the years.

And thank you, dear reader! I hope you take pleasure in using the Cook-Zen pot and the healthful recipes in this book! Enjoy!

CONTENTS

INTRODUCTION

When cookbooks first appeared on the subject of microwave cooking, there was great excitement. Meals prepared in minutes seemed to be the answer for busy households everywhere. The results, however, were often disappointing. Cooking in the microwave required constant stirring, and even then, ingredients cooked unevenly and came out dry and tough. Most microwaveable dishes and utensils, designed for reheating and defrosting, were not sturdy enough to cook an entire meal. There was also the inconvenience of having to take the cookware in and out of the microwave frequently just to stir. Most people gave up on the idea of microwave cooking, but I was convinced there was potential, given the right tools. As a professional chef, I set out to develop the perfect microwave pot. After ten years of experimenting and studying how microwave ovens work, I patented the Cook-Zen.

This "magic pot" cooks vegetables, rice, meat, and seafood perfectly; many of the recipes take just minutes to prepare. Made of thick, high-quality polypropylene, the Cook-Zen heats food evenly and quickly. It also seals in the moisture of your ingredients, so that they cook in their natural juices without a lot of water or oil. This means bolder flavors and more vibrant colors for everything from green beans to salmon. It is also the healthiest method of cooking. Vitamins that would normally dissolve in water are retained in your foods, and the extremely short cooking times also ensure that these nutrients are better preserved. Besides being quick and delicious, Cook-Zen meals are healthier for you, too.

I've developed this collection of recipes especially for the Cook-Zen. Japanese cuisine, well known for its healthy, refined palate, can often be time consuming and difficult to prepare. With the Cook-Zen, however, dishes are done in minutes. These are simple, home-style recipes that you can use for family dinners or when entertaining guests.

For a traditional Japanese meal, select three or five of the dishes in this book and serve them along with rice and soup. When putting together a menu, the Japanese keep the variety of ingredients in mind. Seasonal foods are also featured. Try serving Salmon Marinated With Yuzu (page 160), Tofu with Onion Slices (page 93), and Simmered Eggplant (page 83), for instance. The soup can either be *osuimono*, which is a clear dashi (page 16) or *misoshiru*, a miso-based soup.

You'll notice that the serving sizes are quite modest by American standards. These smaller portions, however, offer more in the way of variety. Having a lot of different ingredients gives balance to a meal, both in flavor and nutrition. If you'd like to prepare larger portions, just double or triple the ingredients in these recipes and cook them in batches. These dishes, the vegetable ones in particular, also make wonderful side dishes. Experiment with these recipes and how to serve them—with the Cook-Zen it's easy to create a personal repertoire.

Machiko Chiba

千葉真知子

5 GOOD REASONS TO USE THE COOK-ZEN

1. It's healthy.
The Cook-Zen cooks ingredients with little or no water, which means valuable vitamins and nutrients that would normally drain off are retained. And because microwave-cooking times are extremely short, more of these nutrients are preserved. Cook-Zen recipes require very little oil, for a naturally low-fat meal.

2. It's easy.
Cook-Zen recipes feature minimal ingredients that are easy to prepare. Once the pot is in the microwave, there's no need to watch over it or stir it constantly.

3. It's fast.
The Cook-Zen works like a pressure cooker, heating foods evenly and quickly. Most of the recipes take under 10 minutes to prepare.

4. It's delicious.
The Cook-Zen brings out the natural flavors of your ingredients. Meat dishes are tender and juicy, and vegetables retain their vibrant color and crispness.

5. It's safe.
Microwave cooking is perfect for teenagers and the elderly. You'll never have to worry about the risk of fire from leaving a pot or an open flame unattended.

1. Top Lid

The top lid has two locks that secure all of the Cook-Zen parts together. Always close these locks before cooking.

2. Middle Lid

The middle lid has patented adjustable steam holes that control whether steam is released or contained during cooking. Trapping steam in the Cook-Zen is what makes ingredients cook faster. When cooking rice recipes, we suggest setting the steam holes to "open." For other dishes, the steam holes should be set to "close."

3. Sieve

Use this sieve to rinse or drain ingredients. The sieve should not be left in the Cook-Zen when microwaving.

Cook-Zen Parts

— 1 —

— 2 —

— 3 —

— 4 —

— 5 —

4. Pot

The Cook-Zen pot is made of thick polypropylene, a material that heats food evenly as it cooks. The pot can also function as a mixing bowl when you are preparing your ingredients.

5. Measuring Cup

The Cook-Zen measuring cup measures 7 fluid ounces. The recipes in this book call for both Cook-Zen cup and regular American cup measurements. Be sure to use the Cook-Zen cup where noted.

HOW TO USE THE COOK-ZEN

Calibrating Your Microwave

There are many different types of microwaves on the market, with power wattages ranging from 800 to 1300 watts. All of the recipes in this book were tested on an 1100-watt microwave, with the power level set to 8, which is medium-high, or 80% of the microwave's total power. If your microwave has a lower wattage, you may need to adjust the power level when using these recipes. Follow the potato test below to determine the best settings for your microwave.

As with all methods of cooking, you will have to experiment with the Cook-Zen and your microwave to get an idea of how quickly things cook. In my own experience, even microwaves of the same model and brand name yield slightly different results. Also keep in mind that continuous use of a microwave without a break can lead to a build up of heat in the machine. This is true for conventional and toaster ovens as well. Just be mindful about shortening cooking times to account for the difference.

Potato Test

Lightly rinse a 1/3-pound potato and, leaving the peel intact, place it in the Cook-Zen. Cover the Cook-Zen and set the steam holes to "close." Place the Cook-Zen in the microwave and set the power level to 8. Heat for 4 to 5 minutes.

To test the potato, pierce it with a fork. It should go in and out of the potato smoothly. The skin should only be slightly wrinkly. If the potato is perfectly cooked, then you should follow all of the recipes as written, using power level 8.

If the potato seems undercooked, then increase the power when using these recipes to level 10, which is high, or 100% of the microwave's power. Follow the recommended cooking times.

Rice & Noodles

Dashi Soup Stock
Bonito Dashi • Kombu and Bonito Dashi

Sushi Tapas
**Sushi Rice • Cucumber Sushi Roll • Smoked Salmon Sushi Roll
Eel Sushi Roll • California Rolls
Pressed Sushi with Cucumber and Whitefish
Tuna Nori Roll • Bite-size Whitefish Sushi**

Onigiri (Japanese Rice Balls)
White Rice • Bonito Onigiri • Shiba-Zuke Onigiri • Salmon Onigiri

Bamboo Rice

Chinese Steamed Rice

Tuna and Ginger Sushi

Barley and Okra

Chirashi Sushi

Daikon Rice

Rice with Sea Bream

Sakura-Ebi Rice

Ume-Kombu Tea Rice

Whitefish-and-Ume Steamed Rice

Harusame Noodle Salad

Noodles with Spicy Miso Sauce

Yakisoba Noodles

Osekihan (Red Bean Rice)

DASHI SOUP STOCK

Many of the recipes in this book call for dashi soup stock. You can either prepare homemade dashi, or use the instant kind, which is available in Asian supermarkets. Though making your own requires a little extra work, with the Cook-Zen it's easy to do, and well worth it. Use thick, fleshy kombu and sliced dried bonito.

BONITO DASHI

Makes 4 Cook-Zen cups of dashi

4 Cook-Zen cups water
3 to 4 thick slices of bonito

1. Place 4 Cook-Zen cups of water inside the Cook-Zen, Cover and heat on medium-high for 4 to 5 minutes with the steam holes set to "close."

2. Add the bonito, cover, and heat on medium-high for 3 to 4 minutes, with the steam holes set to "close." Let stand until cool, without moving the pot.

KOMBU AND BONITO DASHI

Makes 4 Cook-Zen cups of dashi

2-inch section of kombu
4 Cook-Zen cups water
3 thick slices of bonito

1. Place the kombu inside the Cook-Zen along with 4 Cook-Zen cups of water. Let soak for a few minutes. When the kombu begins to soften, using scissors, cut a slit into both sides, an inch apart, so that the kombu can release its flavor. Cover and heat on medium-high for 6 to 7 minutes, with the steam holes set to "close." Be careful not to let the water boil, as that will cause the kombu to release a thick, bitter substance.

2. Remove the kombu from the water and add the bonito. Cover and heat on medium-high for another 1 to 2 minutes, with the steam holes set to "close." Let stand, covered, until cool. Do not move the Cook-Zen or bonito slices inside. If the bonito is pressed or mixed too much, it will give off an unpleasant bitterness.

Note: You can reuse the kombu to make what is known as a "second dashi." This dashi is a good simmering liquid for vegetables and other ingredients. The kombu itself can also be eaten.

SUSHI
TAPAS

The recipes in this sushi tapas section are perfect for entertaining—serve them in any combination you like.

SUSHI
RICE

Makes 5 Cook-Zen cups of rice

2 Cook-Zen cups Japanese white rice
2 1/2 Cook-Zen cups water
1/4 Cook-Zen cup rice vinegar
4 tablespoons sugar
1 teaspoon salt

Preparing sushi rice the traditional way can be unwieldy for the home cook. Cooked rice is cooled down with a hand fan, while it is simultaneously tossed with a mixture of rice vinegar, salt, and sugar. Using the Cook-Zen is much easier—the rice and the sushi vinegar simply cook together. Use this basic rice recipe for all of the sushi tapas in this section.

1. Place the rice in the Cook-Zen, add fresh cold water to cover, and swish the rice around to wash. Drain and repeat several times until the water runs clear. Drain the rice well and place back in the Cook-Zen. Add 2 1/2 Cook-Zen cups water and let soak for 1 hour. Do not drain.

2. When the rice has finished soaking, add the vinegar, sugar, and salt to the same Cook-Zen and mix well. Cover and heat on medium-high for 16 to 18 minutes with the steam holes set to "open." Let stand 3 to 4 minutes. Stir well, replace the lid, and let cool.

CUCUMBER SUSHI ROLL

6 servings

5 Cook-Zen cups cooked sushi rice
1 English cucumber
Small pinch of salt
1/3 cup salmon roe
1/3 cup wasabi green caviar
Chives, cut into 1-inch lengths, for
    garnish

1. Roll the sushi rice by hand into 1-inch thick, 1¹/2-inch long pieces. You will end up with approximately 16 pieces.

2. Using a vegetable peeler, thinly cut the cucumber lengthwise into ribbons, stopping when you reach the seeds. Rub each slice with a very small pinch of salt, to soften the cucumber (be careful not to use too much salt, as it will make the cucumber watery). Roll each sushi piece with a slice of cucumber, then cut the sushi in half crosswise for 32 pieces total. Garnish with salmon roe, wasabi caviar, and chives.

Variation: You can also roll the sushi rice in thinly sliced carrots.

Smoked Salmon Sushi Roll

6 servings

5 Cook-Zen cups cooked sushi rice
1/2 pound smoked salmon
1 English cucumber
1/2 cup salmon roe

1. Roll the sushi rice by hand into 1-inch thick, 11/2-inch long pieces. You will end up with approximately 16 pieces.

2. Using a vegetable peeler, thinly cut the cucumber lengthwise into ribbons, stopping when you reach the seeds. Slice the smoked salmon into long strips. Roll each of the sushi pieces with the smoked salmon, then the cucumber. Cut each piece in half crosswise for 32 pieces total. Top each piece with 1/2 teaspoon salmon roe.

Eel Sushi Roll

Makes 2 rolls, 4 servings

5 Cook-Zen cups cooked sushi rice
1 fillet grilled eel

1. Slice off the tail end of the eel and discard. Place the eel fillet in the Cook-Zen. Cover and heat on medium-high for 20 seconds with the steam holes set to "close." Cut the fillet into three long strips, then cut one of the strips in half.

2. Lay a sushi-rolling mat out on a work surface and place a sheet of cling wrap on top. Using 21/2 Cook-Zen cups of rice, form a 1-inch-thick log that is almost the length of the mat (leave 1/2 inch on either side). Place the rice on the cling wrap and top with 11/2 slices of eel. Using the mat, carefully, but firmly press the eel into the rice.

3. Carefully remove the mat and cling wrap, and slice the roll into 1-inch pieces, wiping the knife blade with a damp cloth between cuts. Repeat with remaining ingredients to make a second roll.

CALIFORNIA ROLLS

4 Servings

4 Cook-Zen cups cooked sushi rice
1 English cucumber
1 carrot
1 grilled eel fillet
1 avocado
2 tablespoons mayonnaise
3 tablespoons ketchup
2 teaspoons kochujang (red chili paste)
1/3 cup orange caviar
1/3 cup white sesame seeds

1.   Cut the cucumber and carrot into 3-inch lengths and julienne them. Cut the eel and the avocado lengthwise into thin slices.

2.   In a small bowl, combine the mayonnaise, ketchup, and kochujang.

3.   Lay the sushi-rolling mat out on a work surface and place a sheet of cling wrap on top. Spread 2 Cook-Zen cups of sushi rice over the cling wrap, leaving the top 1 inch uncovered. Place half of the cucumber, carrot, eel, and avocado on top of the sushi rice, 2 inches from the bottom edge of rice, so that it runs the length of the mat. Top the ingredients with the kochujang sauce.

4.   Gently, but firmly roll the sushi rice. The vegetables and eel should be tightly wrapped in the rice, but the rice itself should not be squashed. Remove the mat and cling wrap. Repeat with remaining rice and fillings, to make a second roll.

5.   Place the orange caviar and the sesame seeds onto separate plates. Roll one of the sushi rolls in the caviar to coat, and roll the other in the sesame.

6.   Slice the rolls into 1-inch pieces, wiping the knife blade with a damp cloth between cuts.

Pressed Sushi with Cucumber and Whitefish

4 servings

5 Cook-Zen cups cooked
    sushi rice
1 English cucumber
1/2 pound sushi-grade
    whitefish, such as sole, fluke, or
    hirame
2 tablespoons green wasabi caviar

1.   Line a 5-inch square mold (or another mold similar in size) with cling wrap and firmly pack in the sushi rice. Very thinly slice the cucumber and fish to the same length as your mold. If the fish is not long enough, you can overlap smaller pieces.

2.   Top the rice with alternating layers of cucumber and fish, pressing them into the rice so that they adhere. Unmold the pressed sushi and remove the cling wrap. Garnish with a mound of wasabi caviar.

TUNA NORI ROLL

4 servings

4 Cook-Zen cups cooked sushi rice
2 sheets nori
2 (1/4-inch thick) strips of English
    cucumber
1/2 avocado, cut lengthwise into 6 slices
1/4 pound sushi-grade tuna, thinly sliced

1.   Lay a sushi-rolling mat out on a work surface and place a sheet of nori seaweed on top. Spread 2 Cook-Zen cups of sushi rice over the nori, leaving 1 inch at the top and 1/2 inch at the bottom uncovered. You should have a flat, even layer of rice.

2.   Place a strip of cucumber, 3 slices of avocado, and half of the tuna 1 inch from the bottom edge of rice, laying the pieces end to end so they run the length of the roll. Start rolling gently and firmly away from you. Set the roll aside. Rinse the sushi mat with water and dry with a cloth. Repeat with remaining ingredients to make another roll. Slice the sushi rolls into 1/2-inch pieces, wiping the knife blade with a damp cloth before each cut.

BITE-SIZE WHITEFISH SUSHI

4 servings

5 Cook-Zen cups cooked sushi rice
1/2 pound sushi-grade whitefish, such as
    sole, fluke, or hirame, thinly sliced

1.   Roll the sushi rice by hand into 16 bite-size balls. Place a slice of white fish on a sheet of cling wrap and top with a piece of sushi rice. Using the cling wrap, wrap the fish around the rice, pressing so that it adheres.

Variation: You can also make this with tuna or salmon.

ONIGIRI

(JAPANESE RICE BALLS)

Onigiri, or Japanese rice balls, are perfect for school or work lunches. Follow the recipe for basic white rice and make either the bonito, shiba-zuke, or salmon onigiri. For a party, try serving all three varieties.

WHITE RICE

Makes 5 Cook-Zen cups rice

2 Cook-Zen cups Japanese white rice
2 1/2 Cook-Zen cups water
Pinch of salt

1. Place the rice in the Cook-Zen, add fresh cold water to cover, and swish the rice around to wash. Drain and repeat several times until the water runs clear. Drain the rice well and place back in the Cook-Zen. Add 2 1/2 Cook-Zen cups water and the salt. Let the rice soak for 1 hour. Do not drain. Cover and heat on medium-high for 15 to 16 minutes with the steam holes set to "open." Let stand for 5 minutes. Follow the directions to make either bonito, salmon, or shiba-zuke-flavored rice balls.

BONITO ONIGIRI

6 servings

5 Cook-Zen cups cooked rice
Couple pinches bonito flakes
1 teaspoon white sesame seeds
6 shiso leaves, roughly chopped
Pinch of salt

1. Mix together the rice, bonito flakes, sesame seeds, shiso, and salt; divide the mixture into 6 portions.

2. Firmly roll each portion into a ball, being careful not to squash the grains of rice.

Shiba-Zuke Onigiri

6 *servings*

5 Cook-Zen cups cooked rice
4 tablespoons finely chopped shiba-zuke
    (Japanese pickles)
1 teaspoon white sesame seeds

1. Mix together the rice, shiba-zuke, and sesame seeds; divide the mixture into 6 portions.

2. Firmly roll each portion into a ball, being careful not to squash the grains of rice.

Salmon Onigiri

6 *servings*

1 (^{1}/4-pound) salmon steak
Pinch of salt
5 Cook-Zen cups cooked rice
1 sheet nori seaweed, cut into 6 strips

1. Place the salmon inside the Cook-Zen, and lightly sprinkle with salt. Cover and heat on medium-high for 1 to 1^1/2 minutes with the steam holes set to "close." Remove the skin and bones, and flake the salmon with your fingers. Mix the salmon with the rice and divide into 6 portions.

2. Firmly roll each portion into a ball, being careful not to squash the grains of rice. Just before serving, wrap a strip of nori around each one.

BAMBOO RICE

Bamboo shoots mark the beginning of spring in Japan.

4 servings

2 Cook-Zen cups Japanese white rice
2 1/2 Cook-Zen cups dashi soup stock
1 sheet (5-inch square) abura-age fried
    tofu
1 small, whole bamboo shoot
2 tablespoons soy sauce
1 tablespoon mirin
Pinch of salt
2 teaspoons sugar

1. Place the rice in the Cook-Zen, add fresh cold water to cover, and swish the rice around to wash. Drain and repeat several times until the water runs clear. Drain the rice well and place back in the Cook-Zen. Add the dashi and let soak for 1 hour. Do not drain.

2. Julienne the fried tofu. Quarter the bamboo shoot, then cut each piece lengthwise into 1/8-inch thick slices.

3. After the rice has finished soaking, add the fried tofu, bamboo, soy sauce, mirin, salt, and sugar to the same Cook-Zen. Cover and heat on medium-high for 15 to 16 minutes with the steam holes set to "open." Let the rice stand, covered, for 3 minutes before serving.

Variation: You can also make this dish with mochi rice. Reduce the amount of dashi to 2 cups and soak the rice for just 30 minutes.

CHINESE STEAMED RICE

32

4 servings

2 Cook-Zen cups mochi rice
2 Cook-Zen cups water
1/2 ounce Chinese dried baby shrimp
2 shiitake mushrooms
1/2 small bamboo shoot
1/2 scallion, finely chopped
1 tablespoon olive oil
3 ounces ground pork
1 tablespoon sake
2 1/2 tablespoons soy sauce
2/3 tablespoon sugar

1. Place the mochi rice in a medium bowl, add fresh cold water to cover, and swish the rice around to wash. Drain and repeat several times until the water runs clear. Drain the rice well and add 2 Cook-Zen cups of water and let soak for just 30 minutes. Do not drain.

2. In a separate bowl, soak the dried shrimp in water until it is soft to the touch; then drain.

3. Cut the shiitake mushrooms and bamboo shoot into 1/4-inch cubes.

4. Place the finely chopped scallion and olive oil in the Cook-Zen and heat on medium-high, uncovered, for 1 minute. When the oil is fragrant, add the rice (including the soaking water), shiitake mushrooms, bamboo shoots, shrimp, ground pork, sake, soy sauce, and sugar to the Cook-Zen. Cover and heat on medium-high for 12 to 13 minutes with the steam holes set to "open." Serve in bowls.

Tuna and Ginger Sushi

6 servings

2 Cook-Zen cups Japanese white rice
2 1/2 Cook-Zen cups water
1/4 Cook-Zen cup rice vinegar
4 tablespoons sugar
1 teaspoon salt
1/2 pound sushi-grade tuna
2 tablespoons soy sauce
1 1/2 ounces ginger
2 tablespoons white sesame seeds
1 shiso leaf, cut into thin strips

1.   Place the rice in the Cook-Zen, add fresh cold water to cover, and swish the rice around to wash. Drain and repeat several times until the water runs clear. Drain the rice well and place back in the Cook-Zen. Add 2 1/2 Cook-Zen cups water and let soak for 1 hour. Do not drain.

2.   When the rice has finished soaking, add the rice vinegar, sugar, and salt to the Cook-Zen; mix well. Cover and heat on medium-high for 16 to 18 minutes with the steam holes set to "open." Remove the Cook-Zen from the microwave, and let the sushi rice stand, covered, for 5 minutes.

3.   Cut the tuna into bite-size cubes. In a shallow bowl, marinate the tuna in 2 tablespoons of soy sauce for 10 minutes in the refrigerator.

4.   Peel the ginger and julienne into very thin strips.

5.   Mix the sushi rice with the ginger and white sesame seeds, and transfer to a serving bowl. Place the marinated tuna on top of the rice, or mix them together. Garnish with shiso chiffonade.

BARLEY
AND OKRA

Japanese pressed barley cooks up to a tender, almost springy consistency, making it the perfect complement to the okra.

4 servings

12 okra
11/3 cups Japanese pressed barley
12/3 cups water
Splash of soy sauce

1.   Wash the okra and place inside the Cook-Zen. Cover and heat on medium-high for 1 minute with the steam holes set to "close." Rinse under cold water until cooled. Cut the okra in half lengthwise, rinse under cold water to remove the seeds, and drain well. Finely chop the okra until it has a sticky consistency. You can also use a food processor for this step.

2.   Place the barley in the Cook-Zen, add fresh cold water to cover, and swish the barley around to wash. Drain and repeat several times until the water runs clear. Drain the barley well and place back in the Cook-Zen. Add 12/3 cups water and let soak for just 10 minutes. Cover and heat on medium-high for 10 minutes with the steam holes set to "open." Let stand, covered, for 5 minutes.

3.   Place the cooked barley in a rice bowl, with the okra on top. Add a splash of soy sauce before serving.

CHIRASHI SUSHI

An elegant, simple dish, chirashi sushi is popular during festivals, when guests stop by, or when relatives get together for a feast. Please use sushi-quality fish!

6 servings

8 shrimp
2 Cook-Zen cups Japanese white rice
2 1/2 Cook-Zen cups water
1/4 Cook-Zen cup rice vinegar
4 tablespoons sugar
1 teaspoon salt
1/2 of a large, sushi-grade squid
1 (1/4-pound) sushi-grade salmon fillet
1 (1/4-pound) sushi-grade tuna fillet
1 avocado
3 tablespoons salmon roe

1. Place the shrimp, with shells intact, in the Cook-Zen. Cover and heat on medium-high for 2 to 3 minutes with the steam holes set to "close." Shell and devein the shrimp and cut each one into three pieces. Set aside.

2. Place the rice in the Cook-Zen, add fresh cold water to cover, and swish the rice around to wash. Drain and repeat several times until the water runs clear. Drain the rice well and place back in the Cook-Zen. Add 2 1/2 Cook-Zen cups water and let soak for 1 hour. Do not drain.

3. When the rice has finished soaking, add the vinegar, sugar, and salt to the same Cook-Zen and mix well. Cover and heat on medium-high for 16 to 18 minutes with the steam holes set to "open." Let stand 3 to 4 minutes. Stir well, replace the lid, and let cool.

4. Cut the squid, salmon, and tuna into bite-size pieces. Score the squid in a cross-hatch pattern. Pit and peel the avocado, and cut into 1/2-inch cubes.

5. Place the cooled sushi rice onto a serving dish and top with the seafood, avocado, and salmon roe.

DAIKON RICE

The leaves of the daikon radish, though often overlooked, are also edible.

4 servings

2 Cook-Zen cups Japanese white rice
2¹/2 Cook-Zen cups dashi soup stock
¹/4 pound fresh daikon radish (about a
    2-inch piece)
1 sheet (5-inch square) abura-age
    fried tofu
A few daikon leaves
1 teaspoon salt
2 teaspoons mirin

1. Place the rice in the Cook-Zen, add fresh cold water to cover, and swish the rice around to wash. Drain and repeat several times until the water runs clear. Drain the rice well and place back in the Cook-Zen. Add the dashi and let soak for 1 hour. Do not drain.

2. Julienne the daikon radish and fried tofu into 1-inch long, ¹/4-inch thick strips. Finely chop the daikon leaves.

3. When the rice has finished soaking, add the daikon radish, daikon leaves, fried tofu, salt, and mirin to the same Cook-Zen. Cover and heat on medium-high for 18 minutes with the steam holes set to "open." Serve in bowls.

RICE WITH
SEA BREAM

4 servings

2 Cook-Zen cups mochi rice
2 Cook-Zen cups water
1 (1/3-pound) sushi-grade sea bream
    fillet, skin and bones removed
Pinch of salt
2 tablespoons white sesame seeds

1. Place the mochi rice in the Cook-Zen, add fresh cold water to cover, and swish the rice around to wash. Drain and repeat several times until the water runs clear. Drain the rice well and place back in the Cook-Zen. Add 2 Cook-Zen cups of water and let soak for just 30 minutes. Do not drain.

2. Cut the sea bream into bite-size pieces. When the rice has finished soaking, add the sea bream to the same Cook-Zen. Cover and heat on medium-high for 13 to 14 minutes with the steam holes set to "open."

3. After heating, remove the Cook-Zen from the microwave and let stand, covered, for 5 minutes. Mix in the salt and white sesame seeds and serve.

UME-
KOMBU
TEA RICE

Ume-kombu tea is made from plum-flavored sea kelp. It is sold in powdered form. Along with the umeboshi, it adds a refreshing, tart flavor to this rice dish.

4 servings

2 Cook-Zen cups mochi rice
2 Cook-Zen cups water
1 1/2 teaspoons ume-kombu tea powder
2 tablespoons finely-chopped pitted
    umeboshi
Pinch of white sesame seeds

1. Place the mochi rice in the Cook-Zen, add fresh cold water to cover, and swish the rice around to wash. Drain and repeat several times until the water runs clear. Drain the rice well and place back in the Cook-Zen. Add 2 Cook-Zen cups of water and let soak for just 30 minutes. Do not drain.

2. When the rice has finished soaking, add the ume-kombu tea. Cover and heat on medium-high for 13 to 14 minutes with the steam holes set to "open."

3. After heating, mix in the finely chopped umeboshi. Garnish with sesame seeds before serving.

Whitefish-and-Ume Steamed Rice

4 servings

2 Cook-Zen cups Japanese white rice

2¹/2 Cook-Zen cups dashi soup stock

1 (¹/4-pound) whitefish fillet, such as
  sole or sea bream

2 tablespoons finely-chopped pitted
  umeboshi

1 tablespoon white sesame seeds

10 shiso leaves, cut into thin strips, for
  garnish

1. Place the rice in the Cook-Zen, add fresh cold water to cover, and swish the rice around to wash. Drain and repeat several times until the water runs clear. Drain the rice well and place back in the Cook-Zen. Add the dashi and let soak for 1 hour. Do not drain.

2. Remove the skin and bones from the fish, and cut into ³/4-inch pieces. Place the fish and chopped umeboshi in the Cook-Zen with the rice. Cover and heat on medium-high for 15 to 16 minutes with the steam holes set to "open." After heating, mix in the white sesame seeds and place the rice in a serving bowl. Garnish with shiso chiffonade.

HARUSAME NOODLE SALAD

Harusame translates as "spring rain." These wonderful mung bean noodles come dried, and upon cooking, turn translucent.

4 servings

2 tablespoons dried kikurage (wood ear mushrooms)
1 cucumber
2 cups bean sprouts
2 ounces harusame noodles
1 Cook-Zen cup water

Dressing
4 tablespoons soy sauce
2 to 3 teaspoons sugar
2 teaspoons sesame oil
1 1/2 to 2 tablespoons rice vinegar
Splash of rayu (hot chili sesame oil)

1. Rinse the kikurage and soak in cool water until soft to the touch; drain well. Cut the cucumber into 2-inch lengths and julienne along with the kikurage.

2. Wash the bean sprouts and place in the Cook-Zen. Cover and heat on medium-high for 1 to 2 minutes with the steam holes set to "close." After heating, rinse the bean sprouts under cool water and drain well.

3. Place the harusame noodles inside the Cook-Zen and add 1 cup of water. Cover and heat on medium-high for 4 to 5 minutes with the steam holes set to "close." Rinse noodles under cool water and drain well.

4. Make the dressing: In a small bowl, combine the soy sauce, sugar, sesame oil, rice vinegar, and rayu.

5. Mix together the noodles, kikurage, cucumber, and bean sprouts. Place in a serving dish and top with the dressing just before serving.

NOODLES WITH SPICY MISO SAUCE

2 servings

1 tablespoon olive oil

3 tablespoons plus 1 teaspoon finely
    chopped scallion

2 teaspoons finely chopped garlic

1/2 pound ground beef or pork

1 teaspoon tobanjyan (spicy miso paste)

2 tablespoons sugar

3 tablespoons soy sauce

1/2 Cook-Zen cup chicken stock

1/4 pound (1 package) fresh ramen
    noodles

3 Cook-Zen cups hot water

1. Place the olive oil, 3 tablespoons finely chopped scallion, and garlic into the Cook-Zen, and heat on medium-high, uncovered, for 1 1/2 minutes.

2. Add the ground meat, tobanjyan, sugar, soy sauce, and chicken stock to the same Cook-Zen and mix well. Cover and heat on medium-high for 4 minutes with the steam holes set to "close." Spoon the sauce into a dish and set aside.

3. Rinse the Cook-Zen and add the noodles along with 3 Cook-Zen cups of hot water. Cover and heat on medium-high for 3 minutes with the steam holes set to "close." Drain the noodles and place on a serving plate. Top with the spicy miso sauce and garnish with 1 teaspoon finely chopped scallions.

YAKISOBA
NOODLES

4 servings

1 Cook-Zen cup bean sprouts
1/4 carrot
1 large cabbage leaf
4 medium shrimp
1 package instant ramen noodles,
　　original soy sauce flavor
1 Cook-Zen cup water

1.　Wash and drain the bean sprouts. Julienne the carrot and the cabbage leaf into 1-inch long, 1/8-inch thick strips (you can also cut them thinly into the shape of your choice). Shell and devein the shrimp, then remove the tails. Leave whole or cut into 1/2-inch pieces.

2.　Break the block of ramen noodles in half and place in the Cook-Zen along with 1 Cook-Zen cup water, bean sprouts, carrots, cabbage, and shrimp. Cover and heat on medium-high for 4 minutes with the steam holes set to "close." Drain well.

3.　Place everything back into the Cook-Zen and add 1/2 of the ramen soup mix packet; mix well. Heat on medium-high for 1 minute, uncovered.

OSEKIHAN
(RED BEAN RICE)

Osekihan is traditionally served on special occasions, as it can be very time-consuming to make. With the Cook-Zen, however, it takes only 30 minutes to prepare, so you can enjoy it anytime.

6 servings

2 Cook-Zen cups mochi rice
5 Cook-Zen cups water
1 Cook-Zen cup dried red beans
    (1/3 pound)
1/8 teaspoon baking soda
Pinch of salt
Pinch of black sesame seeds

1. Place the mochi rice in a medium bowl, add fresh cold water to cover, and swish the rice around to wash. Drain and repeat several times until the water runs clear. Drain the rice well and place it back in the bowl. Add 1 Cook-Zen cup water and let soak for just 30 minutes.

2. While the mochi rice is soaking, lightly rinse the red beans. Place the red beans in the Cook-Zen along with 2 Cook-Zen cups water and the baking soda (which will soften the red beans). Cover and heat on medium-high for 10 minutes with the steam holes set to "close." Drain the beans and replace with 2 Cook-Zen cups of fresh water. Cover and heat on medium-high for an additional 8 to 9 minutes with the steam holes set to "close."

3. Drain the beans, reserving 1 Cook-Zen cup of the red bean water; let cool for 10 minutes.

4. Place the mochi rice and its soaking water in the Cook-Zen, along with the red beans and the reserved red bean water. There should be a total of 2 Cook-Zen cups of liquid in the Cook-Zen pot. Cover and heat on medium-high for 13 to 14 minutes with the steam holes set to "open."

5. Remove the rice to a serving bowl and sprinkle with a pinch of salt and the sesame seeds.

GREEN BEANS

This simple, delicious side dish pairs well with meat or fish.

4 servings

$1/2$ pound string beans, halved
1 teaspoon olive oil
2 tablespoons soy sauce
2 tablespoons dashi soup stock or water
$1^1/2$ tablespoons sugar

1. Wash the string beans and place inside the Cook-Zen. Add all of the remaining ingredients and mix well. Cover and heat on medium-high for 5 to 6 minutes with the steam holes set to "close."

BROCCOLI
WITH SESAME
SAUCE

Sesame seed paste adds a nutty flavor to simple, steamed broccoli. This is a great way to get kids to eat their veggies.

4 servings

1 bunch broccoli (¹/2 pound)
2 tablespoons white sesame seed paste
2 tablespoons dashi soup stock
1 teaspoon sugar
Dash of soy sauce
Pinch of white sesame seeds, for garnish

63

1. Wash the broccoli and cut into florets; place inside the Cook-Zen. Cover and heat on medium-high for 2 minutes with the steam holes set to "close." Rinse cooked broccoli under cool water and drain.

2. In a small bowl, combine the sesame paste, dashi, sugar, and soy sauce; mix well until smooth. Place the broccoli on a serving plate, and top with the sesame sauce. Garnish with sesame seeds.

LILY BULBS

Though still a little obscure, lily bulbs are finding their way onto restaurant menus here in the U.S. You can find them packaged in the refrigerated sections of some Asian supermarkets.

4 servings

2 large fresh lily bulbs (about the size
 of a garlic bulb)
Pinch of Salt

1. Wash the lily bulbs, and remove any dirt or damaged areas with a knife.

2. Place the bulbs in the Cook-Zen. Cover and heat on medium-high for 2 to 3 minutes with the steam holes set to "close." After cooking, the bulb will fall apart and separate into pieces. Season with salt to taste.

JAPANESE WINTER

Tougan, a Japanese winter squash, is often sold in cut wedges. You can identify it by its green peel and white flesh. If fresh lump crabmeat is unavailable, use canned instead.

SQUASH AND CRABMEAT

4 servings

1/2 pound tougan
1/4 cup boiled crabmeat
1/2 cup dashi soup stock
1 tablespoon mirin
Pinch of salt
Dash of soy sauce

1. Lightly peel the tougan and cut into 1-inch cubes.

2. Place all of the ingredients into the Cook-Zen and mix them together. Cover and heat on medium-high for 5 minutes with the steam holes set to "close."

CHILI
POTATOES

For a milder (or spicier) dish, adjust the amount of kochujang. An ice-cold beer is the perfect complement.

4 servings

2 (1/3-pound) yukon potatoes
4 tablespoons soy sauce
2 tablespoons sugar
2 teaspoons kochujang (red chili paste)
Pinch of white sesame seeds, for garnish

1. Wash the potatoes and place them, unpeeled, inside the Cook-Zen. Cover and heat on medium-high for 7 to 8 minutes with the steam holes set to "close." Peel the potatoes and cut into 1-inch cubes.

2. In a medium bowl, mix together the soy sauce, sugar, and kochujang. Mix in the potatoes while they are still hot and toss until well coated. Garnish with sesame seeds before serving.

POTATOES WITH BUTTER-SOY SAUCE

4 servings

2 (1/3-pound) yukon potatoes
2 tablespoons butter
1 1/2 tablespoons soy sauce

1. Wash the potatoes and place them, unpeeled, in the Cook-Zen. Cover and heat on medium-high for 7 to 8 minutes with the steam holes set to "close." Peel the potatoes and cut into bite-size pieces.

2. Place the butter in the Cook-Zen and heat on medium-high, uncovered, for 30 seconds. Add the soy sauce and stir well.

3. Place the potatoes in a serving dish and top with the butter-soy sauce before serving.

WATERCRESS WITH GROUND SESAME SAUCE

4 servings

2 large bunches watercress
1 tablespoon dashi soup stock
1 tablespoon ground white sesame seeds
1^1/2 tablespoons soy sauce
2 tablespoons sugar
2 tablespoons white sesame paste

1.   Wash the watercress and place in the Cook-Zen. Cover and heat on medium-high for 1^1/2 to 2 minutes with the steam holes set to "close." Immediately after heating, place the watercress in a sieve, and run under cool water. Drain well.

2.   In a small bowl, combine the dashi, ground sesame, soy sauce, sugar, and sesame paste; stir until smooth.
Top the watercress with sesame sauce before serving.

TURNIPS WITH SOYMILK

2 servings

2 large Japanese turnips, including
    the leaves
$1/2$ cup soymilk
$1/4$ teaspoon salt
1 teaspoon soy sauce
1 teaspoon mirin

1. Peel the turnips, cut them in half, and place in the Cook-Zen. Cover and heat on medium-high for 2 to 3 minutes with the steam holes set to "close."

2. Add the soymilk, salt, soy sauce, and mirin to the same Cook-Zen and mix well. Cover and heat on medium-high for 30 seconds to 1 minute with the steam holes set to "close."

NAPA CABBAGE AND DEEP-FRIED BEAN CURD

A real comfort food favorite, this dish is a good example of Japanese home cooking.

4 servings

5 napa cabbage leaves (about 3/4 pound)
1 sheet (5-inch square) abura-age
    fried tofu
3 tablespoons soy sauce
3 tablespoons dashi soup stock
1 1/2 tablespoons sugar

1. Cut the napa cabbage and tofu into 3/4-inch thick slices.

2. Place all of the ingredients in the Cook-Zen and mix well. Cover and heat on medium-high for 4 minutes with the steam holes set to "close."

SIMMERED
EGGPLANT

4 servings

3 Japanese eggplants
1 tablespoon olive oil
2 tablespoons soy sauce
1 tablespoon sugar

1. Wash the eggplants and cut them into bite-size pieces. Drizzle the eggplants with olive oil and mix until well coated.

2. Place the eggplants, soy sauce, and sugar in the Cook-Zen; mix well. Cover and heat on medium-high for 4 to 5 minutes with the steam holes set to "close."

ONIONS

Cooking onions in the microwave brings out their natural sweetness.

WITH SESAME MAYONNAISE

4 servings

3/4 pound small onions (about 1 1/2
   inches in diameter)
4 tablespoons ground white sesame seeds
3 tablespoons mayonnaise
1/2 tablespoon water
2 teaspoons mirin

1.   Wash the onions, leaving the peel intact, and place in the Cook-Zen. Cover and heat on medium-high for 4 to 5 minutes with the steam holes set to "close." When cool enough to handle, peel the onions.

2.   In a small bowl, combine the ground sesame seeds, mayonnaise, water, and mirin; mix well.

3.   Serve the onions alongside the sesame mayonnaise, for dipping.

SORAMAME

(FAVA BEANS) *2 servings*

1/4 pound fresh fava beans (in the pod)
Pinch of salt

1. Shell the beans, lightly wash them, and place in the Cook-Zen. Cover and heat on medium-high for 1 to 2 minutes with the steam holes set to "close."

2. After heating, place the beans in a sieve and run under cool water. Peel the outer skin of the beans and lightly sprinkle with salt before serving.

POTATO AND CABBAGE

SALAD

Cabbage adds a nice crunch to this potato salad.

4 servings

2 (¹/3-pound) yukon potatoes
2 to 3 cabbage leaves
1/4 cup mayonnaise
Pinch of salt and pepper
Pinch of sugar

1. Wash the potatoes and place them, unpeeled, in the Cook-Zen. Cover and heat on medium-high for 7 to 8 minutes with the steam holes set to "close." Peel the potatoes and cut into quarters.

2. Wash the cabbage, and cut it into ¹/2-inch thick, 1-inch long pieces. In a medium bowl, sprinkle the cabbage with a pinch of salt and lightly rub it in.

3. In a medium bowl, mix together the mayonnaise, salt, pepper, and sugar. Add the cabbage and the potatoes (while they are still hot) and, by hand, mix into a soft mash.

Variation: If you prefer to use cooked cabbage, place the cabbage in the Cook-Zen and heat on medium-high for 2 to 3 minutes, with the steam holes set to "close."

EGGPLANT WITH MISO SAUCE

This is one of the most popular eggplant dishes in Japan. Keep this versatile miso sauce in mind for other dishes, too. It goes especially well with tofu and fish.

6 servings

1 medium American eggplant
1 tablespoon olive oil
2 tablespoons red miso paste
2 tablespoons mirin
1 tablespoon sugar
2 to 3 shiso leaves, cut into thin strips, for garnish

1. Wash and cut the eggplant into 2-inch thick rounds. You should have 3 pieces. Score the eggplant on one end with a 1/2-inch cross-hatch pattern. Rub the pieces with olive oil.

2. Place 1 piece of eggplant in the Cook-Zen, score-side up. Cover and heat on medium-high for 3 to 4 minutes with the steam holes set to "close." Cook the remaining pieces. After heating, arrange the eggplants on a serving plate, with the criss-cross pattern facing up.

3. In the same Cook-Zen, combine the miso, mirin, and sugar; stir well. Heat on medium-high for 20 seconds, uncovered, then stir again.

4. Top the eggplant with miso sauce before serving, and garnish with the shiso chiffonade.

TOFU WITH ONION SLICES

2 servings

1/2 large block medium-firm tofu
1/4 small onion, thinly sliced
Pinch of bonito flakes
Couple dashes of soy sauce

1. Place the tofu in the Cook-Zen and top with the onion slices. Cover and heat on medium-high for 50 seconds to 1 minute with the steam holes set to "close."

2. Transfer the tofu and onions to a serving plate and top with bonito flakes and a couple dashes of soy sauce.

EGGPLANT WITH GINGER

4 servings

3 Japanese eggplants
Dash of soy sauce
Dash of mirin
Pinch of sugar
Pinch of freshly grated ginger

1. Wash the eggplants and place them unpeeled in the Cook-Zen. Cover and heat on medium-high for 4 minutes with the steam holes set to "close."

2. In a small bowl, combine the soy sauce, mirin, and sugar. Set aside.

3. When cool enough to handle, peel the eggplant and cut into bite-size pieces. Arrange the eggplant on a serving dish and garnish with grated ginger. Top with the soy-mirin sauce before serving.

JAPANESE

Okara, a byproduct of tofu, is very high in protein. Like tofu, it takes on the flavor of the ingredients it cooks with.

OKARA

6 servings

1 tablespoon kikurage (dried wood ear
    mushrooms)
$1/2$ scallion
$1/2$ carrot
1 sheet (5-inch square) abura-age
    fried tofu
$1/4$ pound okara
1 tablespoon olive oil
1/2 cup dashi soup stock
2 tablespoons soy sauce
2 tablespoons mirin
1 tablespoon sugar
Pinch of salt

1. Soak the kikurage in water until soft to the touch; drain and julienne. Cut the scallion, carrot, and fried tofu into 1-inch lengths and julienne.

2. Place all of the ingredients in the Cook-Zen and mix well. Cover and heat on medium-high for 5 minutes with the steam holes set to "close."

SWEET POTATOES WITH LEMON SYRUP

Sweet potatoes are a favorite in Japan.

2 Servings

3/4 pound sweet potato (about 1 potato)
1/2 lemon
1 1/2 tablespoons sugar
1/2 cup water
Pinch of salt

1. Wash the sweet potato and, leaving the skin on, slice into 1/2-inch thick pieces. Cut the lemon into thin slices.

2. Place all the ingredients in the Cook-Zen and mix together. Cover and heat on medium-high for 7 to 8 minutes with the steam holes set to "close."

SIMMERED HIJIKI SEAWEED

4 Servings

1 ounce dried hijiki or 1/4 pound
    of fresh hijiki
1 sheet (5-inch square) abura-age
    fried tofu
1 carrot
2 tablespoons sugar
3 tablespoons soy sauce
3 tablespoons mirin
1/2 cup dashi soup stock

1.   Rinse the hijiki under cool water.
If using dried hijiki, soak until soft to
the touch.

2.   Julienne the fried tofu and carrot.

3.   Place all of the ingredients in the
Cook-Zen and mix together. Cover
and heat on medium-high for 10 to
12 minutes with the steam holes set
to "close."

POTATOES AND BONITO

4 Servings

2 large potatoes or 8 to 10 small baby
    potatoes
1 tablespoon soy sauce
1/2 tablespoon sugar
1 small bag (1/4 ounce) bonito flakes

1. Place washed, unpeeled potatoes in the Cook-Zen. Cover and heat on medium-high for 7 to 8 minutes with the steam holes set to "close." Peel the potatoes and, if using large ones, cut them into 1-inch bite-size pieces.

2. In a medium bowl, combine the soy sauce and sugar. Add the potatoes and toss to coat. Toss again with the bonito flakes.

MEAT & POULTRY

Beef and Ginger Stir-fry
Chicken Wings with Vinegar-Soy Sauce
Chicken with Wasabi-Soy Sauce
Beef and Oyster Sauce with Lettuce
Chicken, Onion, and Shiso Salad
Chicken, Carrot, and Cucumber Salad
Chicken and Vegetables
Teriyaki Chicken
Stuffed Peppers
Sweet-and-Sour Pork
Roast Pork
Ginger Pork
Beef, Potatoes, and Vegetables
Teriyaki Hamburgers
Stuffed Cabbage
Mabo Tofu
Japanese-Style Baked Lamb
Japanese Meatballs
Japanese Roast Beef
Potatoes, Chicken, and Bacon
Stuffed Turnips

BEEF AND GINGER STIR-FRY

4 servings

1/4 pound eye round steak
1 ounce peeled, fresh ginger
3 carrots
1 zucchini
2 king oyster mushrooms
2 to 3 tablespoons soy sauce
1 tablespoon sugar

1. Cut the beef, ginger, carrots, zucchini, and mushrooms into a small dice (1/8- to 1/4-inch cubes).

2. Place all of the ingredients in the Cook-Zen and mix well. Cover and heat on medium-high for 4 to 5 minutes with the steam holes set to "close."

Chicken Wings with Vinegar-Soy Sauce

4 servings

8 chicken wings, tips removed
3 garlic cloves, peeled and halved
1/4 cup soy sauce
1/4 cup rice vinegar

1. Using a skewer or a sharp fork, poke holes into the chicken wings so that the sauce will be well absorbed.

2. Place the chicken wings, garlic, soy sauce, and rice vinegar into the Cook-Zen and mix well. Cover and heat on medium-high for 7 to 8 minutes with the steam holes set to "close."

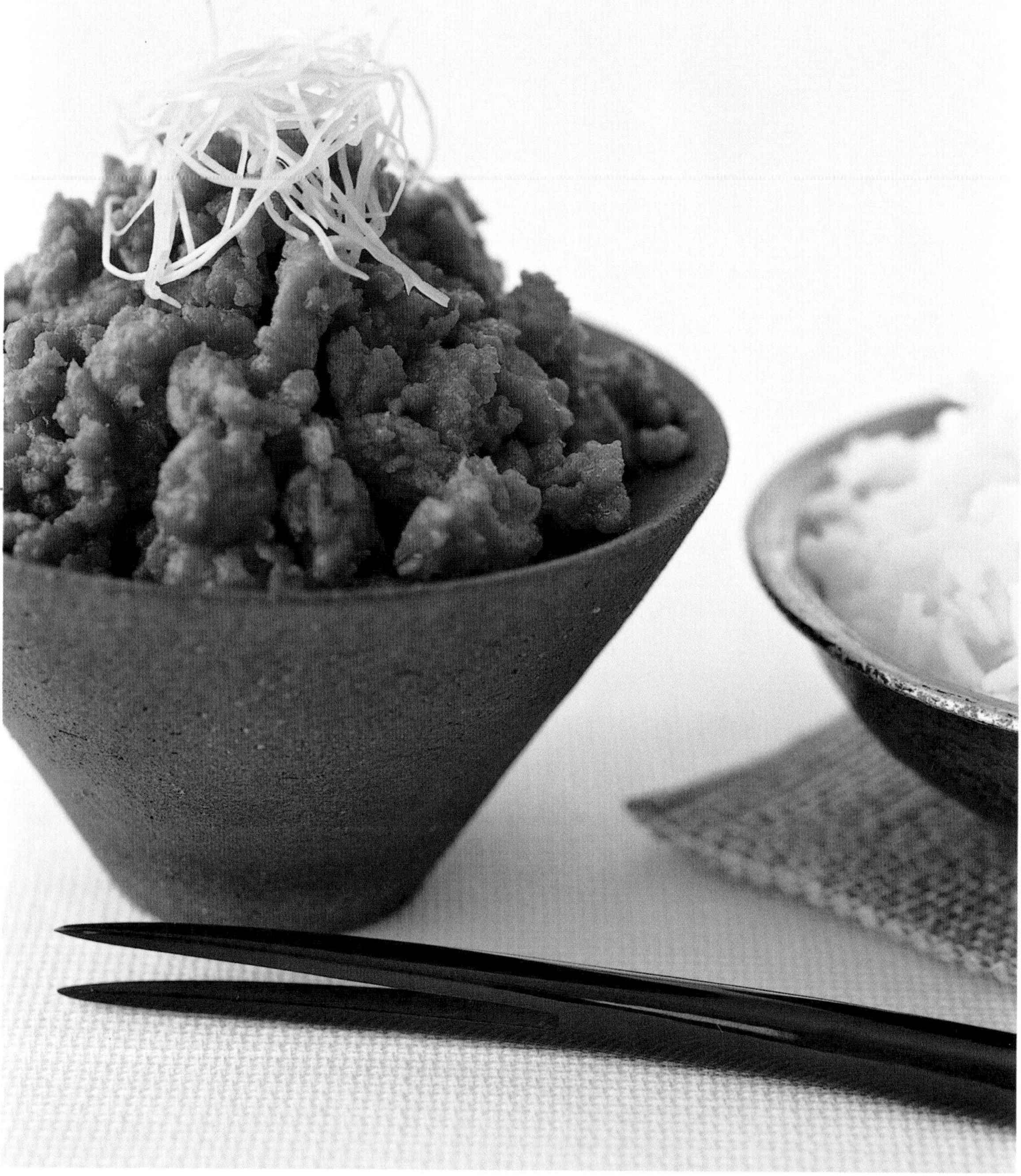

CHICKEN WITH WASABI-SOY SAUCE

Serve this dish over rice or use it as a filling for a sushi roll.

2 servings

1/3 pound ground chicken
4 tablespoons soy sauce
2 to 3 tablespoons mirin
1 teaspoon sugar
1 1/2 teaspoons wasabi

1. Place all of the ingredients in the Cook-Zen and mix well. Cover and heat on medium-high for 3 to 4 minutes with the steam holes set to "close."

BEEF AND

A satisfying, yet light meal.

OYSTER SAUCE
WITH LETTUCE

4 servings

118

1/2 pound sirloin steak
1 tablespoon olive oil
1 tablespoon minced garlic
1 tablespoon finely chopped scallion
1 tablespoon sugar
1 tablespoon soy sauce
1 tablespoon oyster sauce
Red or green leaf lettuce

1. Slice the beef into 1/4-inch thick strips.

2. Place the olive oil, garlic, and scallions in the Cook-Zen. Heat on medium-high for 1 minute, uncovered, until the oil becomes fragrant.

3. Add the beef, sugar, soy sauce, and oyster sauce to the same Cook-Zen; mix the ingredients together by hand. Cover and heat on medium-high for 1 1/2 minutes with the steam holes set to "close."

4. Wrap the beef in lettuce leaves before eating.

CHICKEN, ONION, AND SHISO SALAD

Light dishes, such as this salad, pair well with sake.

2 servings

1/4 pound chicken breast
Splash of sake
1/2 small onion, minced
5 shiso leaves, cut into thin strips
3 tablespoons dashi soup stock
2 tablespoons soy sauce
11/2 tablespoons rice vinegar
Splash of mirin

1. Place the chicken in the Cook-Zen, and sprinkle with sake. Cover and heat on medium-high for 2 to 3 minutes with the steam holes set to "close." Let cool, then shred the chicken into small pieces.

2. Place the minced onion in a bowl and add enough water to cover. Let sit for about 10 minutes, then drain well.

3. In a medium bowl, combine the drained onions, chicken, shiso, dashi, soy sauce, rice vinegar, and mirin. Mix well and serve.

CHICKEN, CARROT, AND CUCUMBER SALAD

This light, refreshing salad is perfect for summer.

4 servings

1/2 pound chicken
    breast
3 small carrots
1 celery stalk
2 small cucumbers
Couple pinches of salt
2 tablespoons rice vinegar
1 tablespoon sugar
1 tablespoon olive oil
Large pinch of dried, shredded kombu

Dressing
2 tablespoons mayonnaise
2 tablespoons mirin
1 tablespoon sugar
1 tablespoon rice vinegar
1 tablespoon olive oil

1. Place the chicken in the Cook-Zen, cover, and heat on medium-high for 3 to 4 minutes with the steam holes set to "close." Let cool, then shred the meat.

2. Slice the carrots, celery and cucumbers (down to the seeds) into ribbons using a vegetable peeler.

3. Rub the vegetable ribbons with a little salt. Place the carrots in a bowl along with the vinegar, sugar, and olive oil. Let marinate for 5 minutes. Soak the kombu in water until it softens, then drain.

4. Make the dressing: In a small bowl, whisk together all of the dressing ingredients until well combined.

5. Mix together the chicken, vegetables, and kombu. Top with the dressing just before serving.

CHICKEN AND VEGETABLES

This is a traditional, home-style Japanese dish. Typically, it requires a long simmer, but with the Cook-Zen, it takes only 12 minutes to prepare.

4 servings

1/3 pound chicken thighs, with skin
1 large carrot
2 shiitake mushrooms
5-inch piece of burdock root (about
    3 ounces), peeled
1/4 cup dashi soup stock
3 tablespoons soy sauce
2 tablespoons mirin
2 teaspoons sugar
8 snow peas

1. Remove the bones from the chicken thighs and cut into bite-size pieces, along with the carrot and mushrooms. Cut the burdock root diagonally on the quarter turn into 1-inch pieces.

2. Place the chicken, burdock root, carrot, mushrooms, dashi, soy sauce, mirin, and sugar in the Cook-Zen. Cover and heat on medium-high for 8 to 9 minutes with the steam holes set to "close." After heating, place the snow peas inside the Cook-Zen and let stand, with the lid on, for 2 more minutes.

TERIYAKI CHICKEN

2 servings

1/2 to 3/4 pound chicken thighs,
    with skin
3 tablespoons soy sauce
2 tablespoons mirin
1 tablespoon sugar
1/2 teaspoon tobanjyan

1. Remove the bones from the chicken thighs and place in the Cook-Zen, skin-side up. Add the soy sauce, mirin, sugar, and tobanjyan. Mix well. Cover and heat on medium-high for 7 minutes with the steam holes set to "close."

STUFFED PEPPERS

For a festive look, use different colored peppers when multiplying this recipe.

2 servings

1/2 pound ground beef
1 tablespoon cornstarch
1 large red, orange, or yellow
    bell pepper
2 tablespoons water
2 tablespoons sugar
5 tablespoons soy sauce

1. In a medium bowl, knead the ground meat well. Add 1 tablespoon cornstarch and knead again.

2. Cut the bell peppers in half lengthwise and remove the core and seeds. Fill with the ground beef.

3. Place the stuffed peppers inside the Cook-Zen, meat-side down. Add the water, sugar, and soy sauce. Cover and heat on medium-high for 8 to 9 minutes with the steam holes set to "close."

SWEET-AND-SOUR PORK

4 servings

Sweet and sour is a delicious, classic flavor combination.

3/4 cup ketchup
Pinch of black pepper
2 tablespoons sugar
1/4 cup rice vinegar
Dash of Asian fish sauce
1/3 Cook-Zen cup water
1/2 pound pork shoulder
1/2 red bell pepper
1 onion
1 carrot
1 small, whole bamboo shoot
1 tablespoon chopped ginger
1 tablespoon olive oil

1. In a small bowl, mix together the ketchup, black pepper, sugar, vinegar, fish sauce, and water.

2. Cut the pork into 1/2-inch cubes. Remove the seeds from the bell pepper and cut, along with the onion, into 1-inch chunks. Thinly slice the carrots into 1-inch lengths. Cut the bamboo shoot in half, and then cut each half lengthwise into 6 pieces.

3. Place the chopped ginger and the olive oil in the Cook-Zen and heat on medium-high, uncovered, for 1 minute.

4. Add the pork, vegetables, and ketchup mixture to the Cook-Zen and mix well. Cover and heat on medium-high for 10 minutes with the steam holes set to "close."

GINGER
PORK

2 servings

1/2 pound pork belly
2 teaspoons grated ginger
2 or 3 tablespoons soy sauce
2 teaspoons mirin
Baby arugula, for garnish

1. Cut the pork into thin, 1-inch long slices and place in the Cook-Zen along with the grated ginger, soy sauce, and mirin; mix well. Cover and heat on medium-high for 31/2 to 4 minutes with the steam holes set to "close." Transfer to a serving plate and garnish with baby arugula.

BEEF, POTATOES, AND VEGETABLES

This is the number one home-cooked meal in Japan.

4 servings

2 yukon potatoes ($^3/4$ pound total),
    peeled
1 onion
3 ounces sirloin beef, thinly sliced
3 tablespoons soy sauce
1 tablespoon mirin
1 tablespoon sugar
$^1/2$ cup dashi soup stock
Pinch of salt
2 ounces frozen green peas, thawed

1. Cut the potatoes into bite-size pieces. Cut the onion into halves and thinly slice them.

2. Place the potatoes, onion, beef, soy sauce, mirin, sugar, dashi, and salt in the Cook-Zen. Cover and heat on medium-high for 13 to 15 minutes with the steam holes set to "close." After heating, place the peas inside the Cook-Zen, cover, and let sit for 2 minutes.

TERIYAKI HAMBURGERS

Served without buns, these teriyaki hamburgers are perfect for a healthy weeknight meal.

4 servings

1/2 onion, chopped
1 teaspoon olive oil
3/4 pound ground beef
1 egg white
1/3 cup Japanese bread crumbs (panko)
Pinch of salt and pepper
4 tablespoons mirin
3 tablespoons soy sauce
2 teaspoons sugar
Drizzle of sesame oil
1 teaspoon cornstarch
Mixed baby greens, for garnish

1. Place the chopped onions and olive oil in the Cook-Zen. Cover and heat on medium-high for 1 minute with the steam holes set to "close." Let cool.

2. In a medium bowl, combine the ground beef, egg white, bread crumbs, salt, and pepper; knead well. Divide mixture into four equal portions.

3. In a small bowl, combine the mirin, soy sauce, sugar, sesame oil, and cornstarch. Mix well.

4. Place the hamburger patties and mirin sauce in the Cook-Zen with the onions. Cover and heat on medium-high for 4 to 5 minutes with the steam holes set to "close."

5. Serve hamburgers topped with sauce from the Cook-Zen and garnished with mixed baby greens.

STUFFED CABBAGE

These mini stuffed cabbages are a lighter take on the classic version.

4 servings

1/4 pound ground pork
4 cabbage leaves
1 cup water
1 1/2 chicken bouillon cubes, crushed
Pinch of salt and pepper
Pinch of sugar

1. Place the ground pork in a medium bowl and knead well; divide into 4 portions.

2. Wash the cabbage leaves, being careful not to tear them, and place inside the Cook-Zen. Cover and heat on medium-high for 3 minutes with the steam holes set to "close." Rinse cabbage leaves under cool water immediately after cooking and pat dry.

3. Place one portion of the ground meat at the bottom of one leaf. Fold in the sides, and roll up the stuffed cabbage. Place seam-side down and repeat with remaining filling and cabbage leaves.

4. Place the water, bouillon, salt, pepper, and sugar in the Cook-Zen and mix well. Add all of the stuffed cabbages, cover, and heat on medium-high for 3 to 4 minutes with the steam holes set to "close."

Mabo Tofu

Tobanjyan is made from a fermented mixture of red chiles, fava beans, and salt. The capsaicin found in chile peppers have been shown to improve circulation, making this dish not only delicious, but good for you, too.

4 servings

1 tablespoon chopped garlic
1 tablespoon olive oil
1 1/2 tablespoons oyster sauce
1 1/2 teaspoons sugar
1 teaspoon tobanjyan (spicy miso paste)
1 tablespoon soy sauce
1 tablespoon cornstarch
1 Cook-Zen cup water
1 small chicken bouillon cube, crushed
1/4 pound ground pork
1/2 large block of medium-firm tofu,
    cut into 1-inch cubes
1/2 onion, chopped
Ito togarashi (shredded dried red chiles),
    for garnish
Cilantro leaves, for garnish

1.   Place the chopped garlic and olive oil in the Cook-Zen and heat on medium-high for 1 minute, uncovered.

2.   In a small bowl, mix together the oyster sauce, sugar, tobanjyan, soy sauce, cornstarch, water, and bouillon.

3.   Add the ground pork, cubed tofu, onions, and oyster sauce mixture to the Cook-Zen. Cover and heat on medium-high for 5 to 6 minutes with the steam holes set to "close."

4.   Place the mabo tofu in a serving bowl and garnish with ito togarashi and cilantro.

JAPANESE-STYLE BAKED LAMB

2 servings

2 small New Zealand lamb chops (2 to
    2^1/$_2$ ounces each), frenched
1 tablespoon soy sauce
1 tablespoon mirin
1 teaspoon sugar
1 tablespoon peeled and grated apple
^{1}/$_2$ tablespoon grated garlic
1 tablespoon grated onion
Pinch of black pepper

1. Place all of the ingredients in the Cook-Zen and mix well. Cover and heat on medium-high for 2 to 3 minutes with the steam holes set to "close."

Note: To prepare 4 lamb chops, increase the other ingredients by 50 percent and cook for 5 to 7 minutes.

JAPANESE MEATBALLS

Many Asian dishes call for tenmenjyan and tobanjyan, so it is good to have these seasonings on hand.

4 servings

3/4 pound ground beef
1 small onion, chopped
1 egg, beaten
Pinch of salt and pepper
1 tablespoon potato starch
2 teaspoons olive oil
1 tablespoon finely chopped garlic
1 tablespoon finely chopped ginger
1 tablespoon finely chopped scallion
2 tablespoons oyster sauce
3 tablespoons soy sauce
1 1/2 tablespoons tenmenjyan
1 teaspoon tobanjyan (spicy miso paste)
3 tablespoons sugar
2/3 Cook-Zen cup water
1 1/2 tablespoons ketchup

1. Place the ground beef in a medium bowl and knead well (the consistency should get stickier as you knead). Add the onion, egg, salt, and pepper, and continue to knead.

2. Form 1-inch balls and lightly coat with the potato starch.

3. Place the olive oil, garlic, ginger, and scallion in the Cook-Zen, and heat on medium-high for 1 minute, uncovered. When the oil becomes fragrant, add the oyster sauce, soy sauce, tenmenjyan, tobanjyan, sugar, water, and ketchup to the same Cook-Zen; mix well. Add the meatballs, and lightly toss to coat them in the sauce. Cover and heat on medium-high for 9 to 10 minutes with the steam holes set to "close."

JAPANESE ROAST BEEF

This Japanese-style roast beef has a subtle, light flavor. If you prefer it slightly sweet, add $1/8$ cup of mirin and a pinch of sugar.

4 Servings

$1/3$ cup soy sauce
2 garlic cloves, sliced
$1/3$ cup rice vinegar
$3/4$ pound round roast

1. Place the soy sauce, sliced garlic, vinegar, and beef, fat-side up, in the Cook-Zen. Cover and heat on medium-high for 4 minutes (rare) or 5 minutes (medium rare) with the steam holes set to "close." Immediately remove the roast beef from the Cook-Zen so it does not continue to cook.

Note: You can reuse the sauce to prepare additional servings.

POTATOES, CHICKEN, AND BACON

4 Servings

2 ($1/3$-pound) yukon potatoes
1 slice bacon
$1/2$ chicken breast (about $1/4$ to $1/3$
    pound)
1 tablespoon olive oil
2 tablespoons minced garlic
1 chicken bouillon cube, crushed
$1/4$ Cook-Zen cup water
Pinch of salt and pepper

1. Peel the potatoes and halve them lengthwise, then cut crosswise into $1/2$-inch slices.

2. Cut the bacon into $1/2$-inch pieces, and the chicken breast into 1-inch cubes.

3. Place the olive oil and garlic in the Cook-Zen and heat on medium-high for 30 seconds, uncovered.

4. Add the potato, bacon, chicken, crushed bouillon, $1/4$ Cook-Zen cup water, salt, and pepper to the same Cook-Zen and mix well. Cover and heat on medium-high for 5 minutes with the steam holes set to "close."

STUFFED TURNIPS

152

4 Servings

4 turnips
1/4 pound ground chicken
1 tablespoon soy sauce
1/2 tablespoon sugar
Pinch of yuzu zest

1.   Peel the turnips and slice off the stem end. Using a spoon, carefully remove 2 teaspoons of flesh from the inside of the turnips.

2.   In a small bowl, combine the ground chicken, soy sauce, sugar, and yuzu zest; knead well. Fill the turnips with the meat mixture.

3.   Place the stuffed turnips in the Cook-Zen. Cover and heat on medium-high for 3 to 4 minutes with the steam holes set to "close."

SEAFOOD

Sardines with Umeboshi
Salmon with Lemon
Salmon Marinated with Yuzu
Shrimp with Lemongrass
Cod with Shiso-Vinegar Sauce
Crab in Chili Sauce
Sea Bass in Spicy Miso
Simmered Sea Bass
Mackerel with Daikon-Oroshi
Clams and Spinach in Soymilk Soup
Steamed Ginger Scallops
Steamed Mussels in Butter-Soy Sauce
Miso-Simmered Mackerel
Sake-Steamed Clams
Steamed Oysters

SARDINES WITH UMEBOSHI

The umeboshi lend a light, tangy flavor to the sardines.

4 servings

4 fresh sardines, cleaned,
    with heads removed
3 umeboshi
1/2 tablespoon rice vinegar
2 tablespoons soy sauce
2 tablespoons sake
1 tablespoon sugar
1 tablespoon mirin
3 tablespoons water

1. Place all of the ingredients in the Cook-Zen and mix well. Cover and heat on medium-high for 5 to 6 minutes with the steam holes set to "close."

2. Place the fish on a serving dish and top with the sauce and cooked umeboshi.

Salmon with Lemon

2 servings

2 (^{1}/4-pound) salmon fillets
Pinch of salt
Juice of ^{1}/2 lemon

Dressing
Juice of ^{1}/2 lemon
2 tablespoons olive oil
2 tablespoons soy sauce
^{1}/2 tablespoon sugar
Strips of lemon peel, for garnish

1. Lightly season the salmon with salt and the juice from ^{1}/2 a lemon. Place inside the Cook-Zen, cover, and heat on medium-high for 3 to 4 minutes with the steam holes set to "close."

2. To make the dressing, in a small bowl, whisk together the lemon juice, olive oil, soy sauce, and sugar.

3. Transfer the salmon to a serving plate. Top with the dressing and garnish with strips of lemon peel.

SALMON MARINATED WITH YUZU

Yuzu peel is high in essential oils, making it very aromatic. For best results, both the yuzu and the grater should be completely dry before zesting.

2 servings

3 tablespoons soy sauce
3 tablespoons mirin
1 teaspoon sugar
2 (3-ounce) salmon fillets
Pinch of green yuzu zest
2 yuzu slices, for garnish

1. In a medium bowl, combine the soy sauce, mirin, and sugar. Add the salmon fillets and yuzu zest. Let marinate for 30 minutes in the refrigerator.

2. Place the salmon and the marinade in the Cook-Zen. Cover and heat on medium-high for 3 to 4 minutes with the steam holes set to "close."

3. Transfer the salmon to a serving plate and garnish with yuzu slices.

Note: You can reuse the sauce to cook more servings.

SHRIMP WITH LEMONGRASS

Serve this dish hot or cold—both ways are delicious.

4 servings

8 jumbo tiger shrimp
1 tablespoon olive oil
1/4 of a scallion, finely chopped
2 garlic cloves
Pinch of finely chopped lemongrass
Dash of Asian fish sauce
1 tablespoon soy sauce
1 tablespoon sugar

1. Shell and devein the shrimp, leaving the tails intact.

2. Add the olive oil, scallions, garlic, and lemongrass to the Cook-Zen. Heat on medium-high for 1 minute, uncovered.

3. Add the shrimp, fish sauce, soy sauce, and sugar to the same Cook-Zen and mix the ingredients together. Cover and heat on medium-high for 3 minutes with the steam holes set to "close."

COD WITH SHISO-VINEGAR SAUCE

Fragrant shiso leaves add a light, delicate flavor to this dish.

2 servings

1 (1/2-pound) cod fillet
Couple pinches of salt
Splash of sake
10 shiso leaves
1/4 cup rice vinegar

1. Cut the cod into bite-size portions and season with a pinch of salt and sake. Place the fish inside the Cook-Zen, cover, and heat on medium-high for 2 to 3 minutes with the steam holes set to "close."

2. Chiffonade the shiso leaves. In a small bowl, combine half the shiso with the vinegar and a pinch of salt.

3. Place the fish on a serving dish and garnish with the remaining shiso. Top with the shiso vinegar just before serving.

CRAB IN CHILI SAUCE

Spicy tobanjyan gives this sauce a kick.

2 servings

2 small live crabs, chilled
Splash of sake
$1/2$ cup tomato ketchup
2 tablespoons sugar
1 teaspoon tobanjyan (spicy miso paste)
$1 1/2$ tablespoons sake
$1/3$ cup torigara soup stock (Asian chicken soup stock)
1 tablespoon olive oil
1 tablespoon minced garlic
1 tablespoon minced ginger
1 tablespoon finely chopped scallion

1. Remove the flap on the underside of the crabs. Rinse and remove the gills. Cut each crab in half, and sprinkle with sake.

2. In a small bowl, mix together the ketchup, sugar, tobanjyan, sake, and torigara stock. Set aside.

3. Place the olive oil, garlic, ginger, and scallion in the Cook-Zen and heat on medium-high, uncovered, for 1 minute until it is fragrant.

4. Add the crabs and the ketchup mixture to the same Cook-Zen and mix well. Cover and heat on medium-high for 5 to 6 minutes with the steam holes set to "close." When the shells are red, the crabs are done.

Variation: You can also use softshell crabs for this dish.

Sea Bass in Spicy Miso

2 Servings

3 teaspoons kochujang
    (red chili paste)
2 teaspoons red miso paste
1 tablespoon soy sauce
1 tablespoon sugar
1/2 Cook-Zen cup water
1 (1/2-pound) sea bass fillet,
    lightly rinsed
4 slices ginger
1 clove garlic, sliced
Ichimi togarashi, for garnish

1.   Place the kochujang, miso paste, soy sauce, sugar, and 1/2 Cook-Zen cup water in the Cook-Zen and mix well. Add the sea bass, ginger, and garlic. Cover and heat on medium-high for 3 to 4 minutes with the steam holes set to "close."

2.   Transfer to a plate and garnish with ichimi togarashi.

SIMMERED
SEA BASS

2 servings

1 (¹/2-pound) sea bass fillet
4 slices ginger
3 tablespoons soy sauce
2 tablespoons mirin
2 tablespoons sake
1 tablespoon sugar

1. Lightly rinse the sea bass and place it
in the Cook-Zen along with the ginger,
soy sauce, mirin, sake, and sugar. Mix the
ingredients together, cover, and heat on
medium-high for 3 to 4 minutes with the
steam holes set to "close."

MACKEREL WITH DAIKON-OROSHI

2 Servings

6-inch piece of fresh daikon
2 (3-ounce) mackerel fillets
3 tablespoons mirin
2 tablespoons sugar
1/2 cup dashi soup stock
1/3 cup soy sauce
Dried red chiles, for garnish

1. Wash and peel the daikon, then grate it. Place in a sieve and let drain.

2. Cut the mackerel into four pieces and place, skin-side up, in the Cook-Zen. Add the grated daikon, mirin, sugar, dashi, and soy sauce; mix together. Cover and heat on medium-high for 4 to 5 minutes with the steam holes set to "close."

3. Transfer the mackerel and sauce to a serving dish and garnish with dried red chiles.

CLAMS AND SPINACH IN SOYMILK SOUP

4 servings

1 pound clams
3 1/3 cups water
3 thick bonito flakes
1/2 teaspoon salt
1/2 cup soymilk
1 small bunch spinach
1 teaspoon soy sauce

1.   Place the clams in a bowl of salt water for 30 minutes to extract any sand or grit. Remove the clams and add to the Cook-Zen along with 4 Cook-Zen cups water, bonito flakes, and salt. Cover and heat on medium-high for 8 minutes with the steam holes set to "close." Discard any clams that haven't opened.

2.   Add the soymilk and spinach to the same Cook-Zen. Cover and heat on medium-high for 1 minute with the steam holes set to "close." Stir in the soy sauce before serving.

STEAMED GINGER SCALLOPS

4 Servings

6 sea scallops
1 tablespoon finely chopped ginger
2 tablespoons finely chopped onion
1 tablespoon finely chopped scallion
Pinch of sugar
Dash of soy sauce
Splash of sake
Chives, for garnish

1. Halve the scallops by placing them on a work surface and cutting into them horizontally. Place in the Cook-Zen along with the ginger, onion, scallions, sugar, soy sauce, and sake. Stir to mix the ingredients, cover, and heat on medium-high for 1 1/2 to 2 minutes with the steam holes set to "close."

2. Remove the scallops and sauce to a serving dish and garnish with chives.

STEAMED MUSSELS IN BUTTER-SOY SAUCE

178

2 servings

1 tablespoon butter
2 cloves garlic, finely chopped
1 pound mussels, washed and scrubbed
1 cup sake
1 tablespoon soy sauce
1 scallion, chopped

1. Place the butter and garlic in the Cook-Zen and heat on medium-high for 1 minute, uncovered. When the butter is fragrant, place the mussels and sake into the same Cook-Zen. Cover and heat on medium-high for 6 to 7 minutes with the steam holes set to "close." Discard any mussels that haven't opened.

2. Stir in the soy sauce and transfer the mussels to a serving dish. Garnish with chopped scallions.

Miso-Simmered Mackerel

2 servings

1 (¹/2-pound) mackerel fillet
1 tablespoon miso paste
¹/2 tablespoon soy sauce
4 thin slices ginger
1 tablespoon sugar
2 tablespoons mirin

1. Cut the mackerel fillet into 4 pieces and place them skin-side up in the Cook-Zen.

2. Add the miso paste, soy sauce, ginger, sugar, and mirin; mix well. Cover and heat on medium-high for 3 to 4 minutes with the steam holes set to "close."

SAKE-STEAMED CLAMS

2 servings

1 pound clams
1 teaspoon butter
1/4 cup sake
1 teaspoon soy sauce
3 sprigs mitsuba, finely chopped,
    for garnish

1. Place the clams in a bowl of salt water for 30 minutes to extract any sand or grit.

2. Remove the clams and place inside the Cook-Zen along with the butter, sake, and soy sauce. Stir to mix the ingredients, cover, and heat on medium-high for 4 to 5 minutes with the steam holes set to "close." Discard any clams that haven't opened. Remove the clams to a serving dish and garnish with finely chopped mitsuba leaves.

STEAMED OYSTERS

2 servings

6 large oysters, such as Blue Point, washed and scrubbed
1/4 cup sake
Dash of soy sauce
Dash of lemon juice
2 tablespoons freshly grated daikon radish
6 chives, finely chopped, for garnish
Ito togarashi, for garnish

1. Place the oysters and sake in the Cook-Zen. Cover and heat on medium-high for 5 to 6 minutes with the steam holes set to "close." If the shells have not opened, heat for an additional minute. Discard any that are still closed.

2. Remove one side of the shell, and place the oysters facing up on a serving plate. Top the oysters with a dash of soy sauce and lemon juice. Lightly squeeze the grated daikon to remove excess water and divide among the oysters. Garnish with chives and a few pinches of ito togarashi.

Note: You can reuse the sake to prepare additional servings.

SESAME YOKAN

6 servings

1/4 ounce kanten (agar agar)
1 Cook-Zen cup water
1 tablespoon mizu-ame (Japanese
    liquid sugar)
1/2 pound canned red bean paste
2 ounces black sesame seed paste
Pinch of salt

1.   Tear the kanten into small pieces and place in the Cook-Zen. Add water to cover and remove any impurities that may float to the surface.

2.   Drain the kanten and squeeze out any excess water. Place in the Cook-Zen and add 1 Cook-Zen cup water. Cover and heat on medium-high for 5 minutes with the steam holes set to "close."

3.   Using a sieve, strain the kanten liquid into a bowl. Add the mizu-ame, red bean paste, black sesame paste, and a pinch of salt to the bowl. Quickly whisk the mixture before it sets and pour into a 3-cup mold. Let cool in the refrigerator until set. Unmold and cut into bite-size pieces.

BROWN SUGAR JELLY WITH ORANGES

4 Servings

3 ounces kurozatou (Japanese powdered
    brown sugar)
1 Cook-Zen cup water
2 teaspoons gelatin powder
1 orange, peeled and sectioned

1.   Place the kurozatou, 1 Cook-Zen cup water, and gelatin powder in the Cook-Zen and mix well. Cover and heat on medium-high for 2 minutes with the steam holes set to "close."

2.   Divide the orange sections among individual 1/2-cup molds, and add the brown sugar mixture. Let cool and place in the refrigerator until the jelly is set.

BAKED PEAR WITH CUSTARD

4 servings

2 small bartlett or anjou pears
1 tablespoon plus 2 teaspoons granulated
    sugar
1 egg yolk
1/3 cup heavy cream
1-inch piece whole vanilla bean
    (or a drop of vanilla extract)

1. Wash, peel, and cut the pears into halves. Place the halves in the Cook-Zen and sprinkle with 2 teaspoons of sugar. Cover and heat on medium-high for 2 minutes with the steam holes set to "close." Remove the pears and set aside.

2. To make the custard, place the egg yolk and heavy cream inside the same Cook-Zen. Mix well using a whisk and add 1 tablespoon of sugar. Split the vanilla bean in half and, using a knife, scrape out the seeds; add to the Cook-Zen. Heat on medium-high for 30 seconds, uncovered. Stir well, then heat again on medium-high for an additional 20 seconds. Continue to cook in 20-second intervals until thick. Stir well until the custard cools down.

3. Place the pears on individual plates. Top the pears with custard just before serving.

Glossary

bamboo shoots
Bamboo shoots are the young, edible shoots of the bamboo plant. They are available in cans, bottles, and vacuum-sealed bags.

bonito flakes
Bonito is a fish, known as *katsuo* in Japan. Fillets are smoked and dried, then grated into flakes of varying sizes and thicknesses. Larger, thicker flakes are used in making stocks, such as dashi, while thinner flakes are used as garnishes.

daikon
Daikon is a large, mild-flavored radish, used in a number of Japanese dishes. The leaves can also be eaten, though stores often remove them, as they discolor quickly when refrigerated.

dashi soup stock
Dashi is a simple soup stock used in many Japanese dishes, including miso soup. There are many types of dashi; the most basic calls for kombu and bonito. Instant dashi can be found in Asian markets, or for a homemade recipe, see page 16.

dried baby shrimp
Dried baby shrimp are available at Asian markets. Though small, they have a concentrated shrimp flavor.

harusame noodles
Harusame noodles are made from mung bean starch. They are sold in dried form, and when soaked in hot water or broth, turn translucent (harusame translates as "spring rain").

Facing page (clockwise from top left): black sesame seed paste; sesame oil; harusame; mizu-ame; dried ramen; fresh ramen; kanten; cooking sake; tenmenjan; ground sesame (white and black); ichimi togarashi; whole sesame; torigara soup stock; dried chiles; red bean paste; rayu; wasabi paste; ito togarashi; Japanese pressed barley; kikurage

hijiki

Hijiki is a thin, black seaweed that is available fresh or dried. Dried hijiki should be soaked before using.

ichimi togarashi

Ichimi togarashi are ground red pepper flakes, often used to season soba or udon noodle soup.

ito togarashi

Ito togarashi (literally, "string chiles") are shredded dried red chiles. Their thread-like shape makes them a beautiful and festive garnish.

Japanese cucumber

Japanese cucumbers are long, slender, and nearly seedless. If Japanese cucumbers are not available, substitute another seedless variety, such as an English cucumber.

Japanese eggplant

Japanese eggplants are long and slender. They have thin skins and tender flesh.

Japanese pressed barley

Japanese pressed barley (*oshi-mugi*) is high in soluble fiber, which helps to reduce cholesterol. Also rich in niacin and iron, it is so nutritious that Japanese families often mix barley with white rice for daily meals.

kabocha

Kabocha is a Japanese pumpkin-shaped squash. It has a dark green peel and orange flesh.

kanten

Kanten, also known as agar-agar, is a seaweed extract that can be used as a food thickener. It is firmer than gelatin and makes a great alternative; it is suitable for vegetarians and it does not require refrigeration.

king oyster mushrooms

King oyster mushrooms, also known as *eringi*, have a trumpet-like shape. The cap is flat and brown, and the stem is white and stout. The mushrooms are firm in texture and meaty.

Facing page (clockwise from top left): medium-firm tofu; firm tofu; okara; abura-age

kiku

Kiku are the edible petals of the chrysanthemum flower. They are available fresh or dried.

kikurage

Kikurage are wood ear mushrooms. They are available fresh or dried. Dried kikurage should be soaked before using.

kochujang

Kochujang is a Korean red chili paste made from fermented soy beans, rice, and hot peppers. It is moderately spicy and slightly sweet.

kombu

Kombu is a type of sea kelp. It is available dried, either shredded or in sheets.

lily bulbs

Lily bulbs can be found in the refrigerated section of some Asian markets.

mirin

Mirin is a sweet rice wine, used solely for cooking.

mitsuba

Mitsuba is sometimes referred to as Japanese parsley; both the leaves and the stem are edible.

mizu-ame

Mizu-ame is a liquid sweetener made from potato starch. It is clear and has a thick, sticky consistency. It is used in Japanese desserts such as yokan.

nori

Nori is dried seaweed that has been pressed into thin sheets. It is most commonly used as a wrapper for sushi, or, when toasted and crumbled, as a seasoning or garnish.

Facing page (clockwise from top left): two kinds of bonito (both used for dashi); nori; hijiki; Chinese dried baby shrimp; sakura-ebi; whole, dried bonito fillet; shredded kombu; large kombu; bonito flakes (used for garnish); medium-size kombu

okara

Okara is the insoluble soy material that is strained from soy milk, in the production of tofu. It is very high in protein. You can find okara in the refrigerated section of Asian markets.

ramen

Ramen is a thin wheat noodle of Chinese origin. It sometimes contains eggs. It is available dried or fresh, in the refrigerated section of some Asian markets.

rayu

Rayu is a spicy chili-sesame oil.

red bean paste

Red bean paste is made from red beans and sugar. The paste is available in cans, jars, or bags.

sake

Sake is a Japanese wine made from steamed, fermented rice.

sakura-ebi

Sakura-ebi ("cherry blossom shrimp") are tiny, translucent pink shrimp. They are available dried or frozen.

sesame seed paste

Sesame seed paste is made from ground roasted sesame seeds. There are two varieties, one made from black sesame seeds (*kuro neri goma*) and the other from white sesame seeds (*shiro neri goma*).

shiba-zuke

Shiba-zuke is a type of Japanese pickle, usually a combination of eggplant, cucumber, and myouga (a type of Japanese ginger). The vegetables are pickled in brine along with purple shiso leaves, ume red vinegar, and sugar, which give the pickles a pinkish-purple color.

shiso leaves

Shiso, also known as perilla, is an herb in the mint family. There are both green and purple varieties; the latter is often used to tint foods pink-purple.

Facing page (clockwise from top left): tougan; fresh wasabi; mitsuba; kabocha; green togarashi; Japanese eggplant; yuzu; bamboo shoot; lily bulb; shiso; Japanese cucumber; king oyster mushrooms

tenmenjyan

Tenmenjyan is a sweet Chinese sauce. Fermented rice and flour are combined and fermented together, resulting in a dark brown color.

tobanjyan

Tobanjyan is a spicy miso paste, made from a fermented mixture of red chili, fava beans, and salt.

tofu

Tofu is made from coagulated soy milk. The curds are pressed into blocks of varying consistencies—soft, firm, and extra firm.

togarashi green chiles

Togarashi green chiles are fresh Japanese hot peppers.

torigara soup stock

Torigara is a Chinese-style instant chicken soup stock, available at Asian markets. To make the stock, dissolve the granules in hot water.

tougan

Tougan is an Asian winter squash with a green peel and white flesh.

umeboshi

Umeboshi are pickled plums, sour and salty in taste. They are naturally brown, but are tinted pink-purple using the purple variety of shiso.

ume-kombu tea

Ume-kombu tea is made from umeboshi-flavored seaweed. It is sold in powder form.

wasabi

Wasabi is a Japanese root with a flavor similar to horseradish. It is most commonly available in powder form, which must be mixed with water before use, or as an already-made paste, available in tubes. Fresh wasabi, though harder to find, is prized for having a sweeter, milder flavor.

yuzu

Yuzu is a citrus fruit, about the size of a lime. Its size and color depend on the season and its degree of ripeness. Yuzu is small and green in the summer and larger and yellow in winter.

INDEX